At David C Cook, we equip the local church around the corner and around the globe to make disciples. Come see how we are working together—go to **www.davidccook.org**. Thank you!

transforming lives together

What people are saying about …

THE MOSAIC COURSE

"I find *The Mosaic Course* to be a great bridge-builder between Christians and people of other religions—it teaches what others believe and what they think we believe. It also reveals the redemptive elements built into other religions that we can relate to in our conversations."

Philip Yancey, Multiple Gold
Medallion–winning author, Editor-
at-large of *Christianity Today*

"We consider it a privilege to partner with the Mosaic Course … Many church programs are striving to find homogeneity in culture, but we look at it as a Mosaic."

Makoto Fujimura, Director, Brehm
Center, Fuller Theological Seminary

"I think this project comes at a time when the Church in the postmodern pluralistic West needs some practical knowledge, encouragement, and insight to help them understand and thereby enter into relationships in ways faithful to the gospel with people from other religions."

Rev. Dr. Greg Waybright, Senior Pastor,
Lake Avenue Church, Former President,
Trinity International University

"The Mosaic Course is for people who are searching for language to communicate with friends the truth of the gospel."

Rev. Dr. Drew Sams, Senior Pastor, Bel
Air Presbyterian Church, Los Angeles

THE MOSAIC COURSE

MATHEW P. JOHN

THE MOSAIC COURSE

UNDERSTANDING WORLD RELIGIONS
FROM A CHRISTIAN PERSPECTIVE

DAVID C COOK

transforming lives together

THE MOSAIC COURSE
Published by David C Cook
4050 Lee Vance Drive
Colorado Springs, CO 80918 U.S.A.

Integrity Music Limited, a Division of David C Cook
Brighton, East Sussex BN1 2RE, England

The graphic circle C logo is a registered trademark of David C Cook.

The website addresses recommended throughout this book are offered as a
resource to you. These websites are not intended in any way to be or imply an
endorsement on the part of David C Cook, nor do we vouch for their content.

All Scripture quotations are taken from the New American
Standard Bible®, copyright © 1960, 1995 by The Lockman
Foundation. Used by permission. (www.Lockman.org.)

ISBN 978-0-8307-8075-4
eISBN 978-0-8307-8100-3

© 2020 Mathew P. John
First edition published by Focus Infinity Press © 2017
Mathew P. John, ISBN 978-0-9867-0597-7.

The Team: Michael Covington, Jeff Gerke, Megan Stengel,
Nick Lee, Jon Middel, Susan Murdock
Cover Design: James Hershberger

Printed in the United States of America
Second Edition 2020

1 2 3 4 5 6 7 8 9 10

011020

COURSE CONSULTANTS

Dr. John P. Bowen
(Christianity)

Dr. Thomas (In-Sing) Leung
(Buddhism)

Dr. Joshua Thambiraj
(Hinduism)

Dr. Mona Scrivens
(Sikhism)

Muhammad (Sam) Nasser
(Islam)

Maria Short
(Judaism)

Dan Stephenson
(Secular Humanism)

CONTENTS

INTRODUCTION

The Mosaic Course is an educational platform that explores the foundational belief systems and practices of world religions from a Christian perspective.

The course package consists of *The Unknown God* (book), *The Mosaic Course* study guide (which you hold in your hands), and seven audiovisual modules available online at www.themosaiccourse.org.

Our learning outcome goals for this set of materials:

- You will understand the uniqueness and significance of the Christian faith in the

context of other religious traditions and
worldview assumptions.

- You will discover redemptive revelations
  ingrained in major world religions.

- You will learn to communicate the gospel
  with your neighbors of other faiths in a
  culturally sensitive fashion.

The key objective of the Mosaic Course is to equip
Christians to proclaim the singular and distinct perfection of
Christ in a pluralistic society, while also paying due respect to
people of other religious faiths and worldview assumptions.

The course functions as a personal enrichment pro-
gram for individual Christians, a small group curriculum
for congregations, and an introductory course in world
religions for educational institutions.

HOW TO USE THE STUDY GUIDE

This Study Guide is a companion volume to *The Unknown
God* book and the Mosaic Course audiovisual modules.

We recommend you follow these steps:

- Register for the course online at www.themosaiccourse.org.

- Watch the video lectures for each module.

- Review the Key Points in this Study Guide.

- Read the suggested chapters from the book, *The Unknown God.*

- Answer the Reflection Questions in this Study Guide.

- Complete the Exercises in this Study Guide.

- Take the online test.

- Apply for the Mosaic Certificate once you pass all the modules.

We strongly recommend that you join a **Mosaic Group** to discuss the reflection questions and practical exercises. In addition to what you find in this Study Guide, please visit our website for additional resources that will help you organize a Mosaic Group.

THE MOSAIC GROUP

A Mosaic Group is a small group community committed to meet on a periodic basis to study the Mosaic Course modules in a group setting. The purpose of the group is to enhance the learning experience through discussions, exercises, and supplementary reading materials.

STARTING A MOSAIC GROUP

STEP 1: All members should register for the Mosaic Course online at www.themosaiccourse.org.

STEP 2: Order a copy of 1) *The Unknown God* and 2) this Study Guide for each member of the group.

STEP 3: Identify leaders and helpers for the group and follow the guidelines suggested below in the section Scheduling a Mosaic Group.

NEED HELP?

You can post all your questions at the Mosaic Help Desk, and they will be answered in an upcoming Q&A Webinar.

You may also invite one of our speakers to do a **Mosaic Live** seminar at your location.

PROMOTING A MOSAIC GROUP

- Generally, people outside the church community are also interested in learning about world religions. Therefore, it is a good idea to advertise the group in public platforms (such as newspapers, local clubs, coffee shops, TV/radio stations, etc.).

- Customize the following graphic files available for download at our website for promotional purposes:

  Mosaic Group Poster

  Mosaic Group Flyer

  Mosaic Group Power Point

  Mosaic Group Social Media Post

  Mosaic Group Video Trailers

  Mosaic Group Bulletin Blurb

  Mosaic Group Personal Invitation Letter or Email

- It is ideal to launch the Mosaic Group with a Mosaic Live seminar. You may collaborate with other congregations in your neighborhood to maximize resources and logistics for the seminar.

SCHEDULING A MOSAIC GROUP

A group is more effective when it is smaller in size. It is best to limit the number of members to a maximum of twelve.

It is important for the leader to discern the type of people he or she should admit into the group. Ideally, the group should be affiliated with a church, school, or other institution.

As is often said, "Consistency is the key" to the success of a group. It is important for the attendees to be regular and on time to the meetings. Always remember to finish the group on time. If people express genuine interest to continue the discussions, the leader may choose to extend the time, but only after officially closing the group.

MEAL

It is a good idea to start the group with a meal. It creates an atmosphere conducive to friendly discussions, even if there are people from more than one faith present.

SCRIPTURE READING

Please remember that the suggested Scripture verses are meant only for reading, not necessarily for discussion during your meeting time.

Each chapter of the book *The Unknown God* opens with a passage from different religious texts. You may also choose to read these excerpts along with the Scripture verses.

PRAYER

Prayer should be brief and sensitive to people of other religious faiths, if any are present in the group.

WATCH

Ideally, the participants should preview each video at home. But it is also important for the group to review them together in the meeting.

GROUP DISCUSSION

Limit the discussions to the reflection questions listed in this Study Guide.

Since the video modules are kept short to respect meeting time duration, most questions can be fully answered only after reading the corresponding chapters in *The Unknown God*.

The discussions should *not* turn into a Q&A session where one person attempts to answer the questions raised by the others.

Instead of trying to answer a difficult question, the leader should note it and post it at the Mosaic Help Desk.

EXERCISE

Share your experiences as you work through the exercises suggested in this Study Guide.

INTERCESSORY PRAYER

Take time to pray for your neighbors of other faiths and
other specific needs shared in the group.

REDISCOVERING RELIGION IN A MULTICULTURAL MOSAIC

"How dare you say that Jesus is the only way to God? What an intolerant and insensitive claim to make in our pluralistic world!"

This is a criticism often leveled against Christians who dare to believe that their faith is somehow unique and worthy to be shared with others. In the multicultural society we live in, most people believe all religions are equal, simply providing different paths to the same spiritual destination.

In such a context, many Christians find themselves wondering, "My neighbors of other religions are just as good as, if not better than, my fellow church members. Who am I to say that their faith is any less than mine? I would rather keep quiet and not risk offending others."

Is there a way to affirm the biblical notion that Jesus is the only way to God without being branded as intolerant or arrogant? Is it possible to believe in the uniqueness and significance of Christian convictions while also paying due respect to people of other religious traditions and worldview assumptions? These are some of the crucial questions we are going to address in the Mosaic Course.

In the seven modules of the course, we will explore the foundational belief systems and practices of six major living religions of the world: Hinduism, Buddhism, Sikhism, Islam, Judaism, and Christianity.

We will discover that the followers of the non-Christian religions possess a respectful, if not reverential, understanding of the same Christ the Christians worship as the Son of God. The realization of this fact will challenge us to revise our gospel communication by starting conversations with "the Jesus they know" and then inviting them to see "the Jesus we know."

DEBATES AND DIALOGUES

Our postmodern, pluralistic world is a marketplace of ideas. All religions are considered legitimate expressions of truth, and the term *spirituality* has become a cultural category that describes subjective experiences. Any attempt to proclaim the singular and distinct perfection of the gospel is immediately associated with negative stereotypes such as cultural imperialism, intolerance, and even bigotry.

Many Christians in conservative circles are familiar with the term *apologetics*, the defense of faith. The purpose of apologetics is to equip Christians "to make a defense to everyone who asks to give an account for the hope that is in [us]" (1 Peter 3:15). Apologetics operates by appealing to evidence and reason, articulating the authenticity of the Christian faith in public platforms.

An obvious problem with apologetics is its complexity. One needs to possess a considerable level of intellectual prowess and biblical knowledge to apply apologetic methods in ordinary conversations. This is why many churches rely on professional apologists.

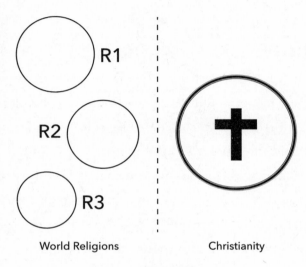

World Religions   Christianity

Figure 1. Apologetic Debates

Apologetics starts by drawing a line of demarcation between Christianity and other religions (R1, R2, R3, etc.), invariably creating a divide between us and "the other." Apologetic debates, therefore, are more confrontational than invitational. They thrive on hostile denunciation and unsympathetic criticism of other faiths, making it practically impossible to build bridges.

An alternative approach to engaging world religions, predominantly popular in the progressive circles, is that of interfaith dialogues. Christianity and other religions come together at a round table to listen to and learn from one another. Each of them overlaps with Christianity in different measures, and the dialogue will be focused primarily on these areas of intersection. Depending on the size of the overlap, certain religions can be better dialogue partners than others.

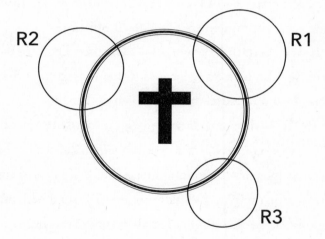

Figure 2. Interfaith Dialogues

A dialogue, by definition, is more conversational than confrontational. This is a step in the right direction. In order to facilitate the dialogue, however, we will have to steer clear from theological propositions that are central to each faith. Therefore, interfaith dialogues tend to focus mostly on ethical and moral aspects of religion, with an intentional disregard for dogmas and doctrines.

Interfaith dialogues have enjoyed increased popularity in our postmodern world, but they often succumb to the demands of political correctness and lose any ability to communicate the gospel with conviction. "A religion which has given up claiming uniqueness, one might fairly say, is of no special interest," says Jürgen Moltmann,[1] one of the most prominent theologians of our time.

If we believe that the gospel is to be preached across the world, we also have to believe that the message it contains is unique and decisive—perhaps even exclusive.

The Bible does not allow us to compromise the fact that the Christ-event was a decisive moment in history, which was crucial for the salvation of humankind. While it is commendable on our part to explore common ground with other religions and work with them on humanitarian concerns, we should never forget the fact that the true mandate of the church is to preach "Christ crucified" (1 Corinthians 1:23). The heart of the gospel is the cross of Christ. Any conversation that deliberately avoids this central truth is, in Jesus' language, like salt that has lost its flavor (see Luke 14:34).

This brings us to the heart of our predicament: interfaith dialogues are preoccupied with the task of finding common ground between different religions, focusing only on the superficial similarities they might share. Apologetic debates, on the other hand, obsess over philosophical discourses and turn into contentious and controversial arguments.

The Mosaic Course introduces a different approach to the conversation—a "redemptive method" that attempts to be both culturally sensitive and theologically sound at the same time.

A REDEMPTIVE APPROACH

The apostle Paul once addressed a pluralistic society at Mars Hill in Athens (Acts 17:16–34). The worldview of his audience was a hodgepodge of ideas ranging from Stoicism, which opted for an escapist withdrawal from the world, to Epicureanism, which called for a hedonistic immersion into it. It was, in many ways, a microcosm of today's global village.

Although the idols erected at every corner of the city provoked Paul's spirit, he began his sermon not by condemning idolatry, but by affirming their zeal for God. Pointing to the altar of an idol marked *Agnostos Theos* (the unknown god), Paul said, "What you worship in ignorance, this I proclaim to you" (Acts 17:22–34). He was not preaching a new religion. Instead, he was revealing the hidden God embedded in their own religious cult. The unknown god of the Athenians suddenly became a signpost that pointed to the God of the Bible.

What Paul uses here is a strategy we might call "reverse hermeneutics." A typical sermon begins with a Scripture passage, exegetes it, and ends with its application in the culture. But Paul reverses this process at Mars Hill: he starts with the culture, identifies a redemptive element in it, and bridges the culture to the Scripture.

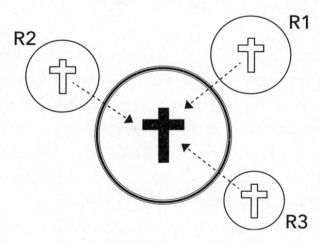

Figure 3. A Redemptive Approach

The Mosaic Course follows the same strategy. In it, we attempt to redeem the unknown god embedded deep within the theological center of various religions. The multifaceted depictions of a "Christ figure" in religions R1, R2, and R3 become pathways that lead the people of those religions to its historical fulfillment in the person of Jesus Christ, as revealed in the Bible.

The task of evangelism then becomes simple and straightforward. When we share the gospel with our neighbors of other faiths, we are not selling them a new religion—we are introducing them to a person who embodies the fullness of their own religious experiences and expectations.

In our journey through six major world religions in the Mosaic Course, we will encounter the silhouette of the unknown god emerging from the deep recesses of their sacred scriptures.

We will meet the *avatar* in the Hindu pantheon, an embodied god with a salvific mission. In the Buddhist universe, we will see the *bodhisattva*, an enlightened teacher who has vowed to rescue humanity from a suffering world. In Sikhism, we will witness God revealing Himself to the world through His Word. We will come face to face with the Jesus of Islam, the only human ever to enter the world without a father and the only prophet who is going to come back again to reestablish God's domain on the earth.

We will explore the Jewish texts struggling to reconcile the conflicting portrayals of the Messiah as both triumphant king and suffering servant.

In the end, we will discover that God's redemptive plan for the world through Christ has been unfolding in every culture and in every religion since the beginning of time. This discovery will help us appreciate the wide spectrum of spiritual experiences we find in our multicultural mosaic without compromising the singular and distinct perfection of the gospel.

MODULE 1

THE ONLY WAY
TO GOD

OBJECTIVE

The purpose of this module is to examine the claims of exclusivity in major world religions through the lens of ideological frameworks such as pluralism, universalism, and exclusivism. We will also compare and contrast the foundational worldviews of six major living religions and explore the traces of general revelation available in their sacred narratives.

SCRIPTURE

Acts 17:22–31

WATCH

The Only Way to God
(Module 1: The Mosaic Course)

KEY POINTS

- Human beings are "religious animals." We are wired to worship something bigger than ourselves. When we stop worshipping God, we will start worshipping ourselves.

- *Pluralism* (analogy: the blind men and the elephant): This view says that different religions perceive different aspects of the Truth. We need to listen to and learn from one another because *no one* gets it right.

- *Universalism* (analogy: how to climb a mountain through different trails): All religions reach the same destination irrespective of the paths they have chosen. We should not interfere with others' religious beliefs, because *everyone* gets it right in the end.

- *Exclusivism* (analogy: the only way through a maze): Truth, by definition, is exclusive. There is only one way that leads to the absolute Truth and only *one* religion gets it right.

- Most religions are *exclusivistic* at their theological center.

- There are only six religions that can be classified as major "living" world religions. Hinduism, Buddhism, and Sikhism are categorized as Eastern religions, and Judaism, Christianity, and Islam as Abrahamic religions.

- Theological frameworks of Eastern religions range all the way from animism to non-theism, while Abrahamic religions follow a strict monotheistic code.

- Eastern religions operate on a mythical timeline, but in Abrahamic religions, God interrupts human history.

- Abrahamic religions conceptualize the cosmos in such a way that God and humans are distinct entities separated from each other by the "sins" of humanity. The ultimate goal of Eastern religion is to bridge the gap between God and humans.

- In Eastern religions, the divine and the human are not considered separate beings. Any apparent distinction between them is caused by a phenomenon called *maya* (illusion). The realization of this truth is what leads us to "enlightenment."

- World religions possess a respectful, if not reverential, understanding of Jesus Christ. The Jews consider Him a rabbi who claimed to be their Messiah; the Muslims, a prophet; the Sikhs, a guru or *sant*; the Buddhists, a bodhisattva; the Hindus, an avatar.

- Paul's Mars Hill sermon (Acts 17:22–31) suggests that there are "Christ figures" in other religions that may function as missiological bridges to invite people to move from "the Jesus they know" to "the Jesus we know."

- The theory of general revelation suggests that God has not left Himself without witness (Acts 14:17) and continues to reveal Himself through nature, conscience, and even through world religions. But the *particular* revelation comes only through the providential grace of God in Jesus Christ.

- The Bible affirms that there is only one way to God and that way is Jesus, but it is plausible that there is more than one way to *Jesus*. There are Christ figures in other religions that have the potential to lead people to the Jesus of the Bible, even through unconventional ways.

- It is therefore possible for Christians to appreciate the genuine spiritual experiences of people of other religions, while also affirming the uniqueness of the gospel and the singular and distinct perfection of the Christian faith.

READ

"Following the Star"
Chapter 1, *The Unknown God*

"The True Myth"
Chapter 8, *The Unknown God*

REFLECTION QUESTIONS

1. How would you respond to the statement, "All religions are exclusivistic at their theological center"?

2. How is the nature of divinity and humanity distinguished in Eastern and Abrahamic religions?

3. What are some of the redemptive roles played by "outsiders" in the biblical narrative?

4. How does Paul's Mars Hill sermon differ from his other missionary discourses?

5. What is general revelation? How is it different from particular revelation?

EXERCISE

Ask people of different ethnic, cultural, and religious backgrounds what they think about Jesus Christ. How do their perceptions of Jesus differ from yours?

What are some examples of general revelation you observe in your everyday life?

MODULE 2

UNDERSTANDING HINDUISM

OBJECTIVE

This module outlines the theological and cosmological frameworks of Hinduism from a Christian perspective. It also examines how Jesus appears in the religious imagination of the Hindus as a yogi, as an avatar, and as a cosmic sacrifice.

SCRIPTURE

Philippians 2:5–8

WATCH

Understanding Hinduism
(Module 2: The Mosaic Course)

KEY POINTS

- Hinduism is a religion with no known founder. People south of the Hind River in India were first classified as Hindus by Persian invaders.

- Hinduism, therefore, is not one religion— it is an amalgamation of various belief systems and religious practices that existed in the geographical region south of the Hind River.

- The Hindu scriptures are classified into *Sruthi* (what is heard or revealed) and *Smrithi* (what is remembered). The four Vedas (Rig, Sama, Yajur, Atharva) of the Sruthi tradition are the most authoritative scriptures of Hinduism. However, Mahabharata and Ramayana, epics in the Smrithi tradition, are more popular than the Vedas among the Hindus. The *Bhagavad Gita*, an excerpt from the Mahabharata, is considered the most versatile of all Hindu scriptures.

- Hinduism is founded on the principle of *Sanatana Dharma*, defined by the phrase: "That which exists is One: sages call it by various names." In that sense, it can be considered a monotheistic or monistic religion.

- The God figure in Hinduism is the Brahman—the Universal Soul—best expressed as the sound "OM."

- The supreme goal of Hinduism is the union between the individual soul (*atman*) and the Brahman. The process of achieving this union is called *Yoga* (yoked together). The way of accomplishing this union is called *marga* (path).

- Raja Yoga/Marga (way of discipline) uses physical postures and meditation techniques to boost the psychic energy of the atman to align itself with the Brahman.

- Karma Yoga/Marga (way of action) uses disinterested action (*nishkama karma*) to peel off the layers of ego until there is no barrier left to separate atman from Brahman.

- Jnana Yoga/Marga (way of knowledge) believes in *Nirguna* Brahman, an impersonal god with no attributes. The union is achieved by exercising our intellect (mindful meditation) to eliminate ignorance (*avidya*).

- Bhakti Yoga/Marga (way of devotion), the most popular form of Hindu religious practice, proposes the idea of *Saguna* Brahman (a god who has personal attributes), often called Ishvara or Bhagvan. The union with Ishvara is achieved through love and devotion.

- The one god, Ishwara, manifests himself as three distinct personal gods (the *Trimurthy*): Brahma (creator), Vishnu (sustainer), and Shiva (destroyer).

- The Brahma is depicted as a god with four heads faced in four different directions. Shiva is often portrayed as half man and half woman (*arthanariswaran*). The female side of Shiva is called Shakti. She appears as Shiva's wife, Parvati, as well as two other goddesses—Durga and Kali.

- Vishnu enters the world when evil overcomes good and the harmony of the world is threatened. His descent into the world is called *Avatar* (incarnation).

- The ten most popular descents of Vishnu are collectively called *Dasavatara*. Rama and Krishna are the most popular and commonly worshipped avatars.

- The final avatar (Kalkin) is going to come at the end of this age. He is described in language similar to that of the apocalyptic savior figure in the book of Revelation. He is going to destroy the existing world and initiate a new epoch called the *Satya Yuga* (the age of truth).

- The avatars of Hinduism came to destroy sinners and save the righteous. But Jesus came to save sinners, not destroy them. He will come back again as the final avatar to establish the reign of God in a new world.

- In Jnana Yoga, Jesus is often considered to be a *yogi* (one who has achieved the ultimate union with Brahman). In Bhakti Yoga, Jesus is considered to be an avatar (the manifestation of God in human flesh).

- *Yajna* (sacrifice) is considered the link between the human and the divine in Hinduism. Vedas talk about Prajapati, a god who performed a cosmic sacrifice with his own body and became immortal after experiencing death. There are many parallels between the Prajapati sacrifice in Vedas and the atoning sacrifice of Jesus Christ on the cross.

READ

"The Descent of God"
Chapter 2, *The Unknown God*

REFLECTION QUESTIONS

1. What would be your response to a Christian from India who regards himself/herself also as a Hindu?

2. Is yoga nothing more than a physical exercise routine? Why or why not?

3. Is Hinduism a monotheistic religion?

4. How is "the Jesus avatar" of the Bible different from the avatars of Hinduism?

5. Comment on Sadhu Sunder Sing's analogy, "Hinduism has been digging channels. Christ is the water to flow through these channels."

EXERCISE

Watch the film *Avatar* (2009). Observe how it reflects the theological framework of avatar in Hinduism and the doctrine of incarnation in Christianity.

Gather pictures of various Hindu deities from the Internet. Who are they and what are they known for?

MODULE 3

UNDERSTANDING BUDDHISM

OBJECTIVE

This module explores the story of Buddha and introduces the key concepts of the Buddhist philosophy. It also illustrates how Jesus is perceived as one of the bodhisattvas who came down from the realm of *nirvana* (ultimate bliss) to *samsara* (material world) to help others attain enlightenment.

SCRIPTURE

Ecclesiastes 1:12–18; 12:9–14

WATCH

Understanding Buddhism
(Module 3: The Mosaic Course)

KEY POINTS

- Buddhism is a religion founded by Siddhartha Gautama (566–486 BC), a prince of ancient India.

- Buddha is not God. The word *buddha* means "the awakened or enlightened one." All sentient beings are endowed with "Buddha nature" and all have the potential to become Buddhas.

- The Four Noble Truths are considered the essence of Buddha's teachings, detailed in the *Dharma Chakra* (*The Wheel of Doctrine*).

    The truth of Suffering (*Dukkha*): Life is suffering.

    The truth of Arising (*Samudaya*): Suffering is caused by desire.

    The truth of Cessation (*Nirodha*): Suffering does have an end.

    The truth of the Path (*Marga*): A path that leads to the end of the suffering, which is known as the middle way.

- The middle way is "one of moderation in which the appetites are neither denied nor indulged to excess." It is achieved through the eightfold path: (1) Right View, (2) Right Resolve, (3) Right Speech, (4)

Right Action, (5) Right Livelihood, (6) Right Effort, (7) Right Mindfulness, and (8) Right Meditation.

- Buddhism does not allow for the existence of God or of personal soul. Buddhist philosophy is often summarized by the term *shunya* (emptiness), meaning that everything is impermanent and empty of identity.

- Sentient beings are created by five *skandhas* coming together to create an illusion, which we perceive as life. These five are physical body (*rupa*), sensation (*vedana*), perception (*samjna*), cognition (*sankhara*), and consciousness (*vijnana*).

- The ultimate liberation in Buddhism is *nirvana*, which literally means "quenching" or "blowing out." In the realm of nirvana, self is extinguished and individual consciousness merges into the universal consciousness.

- Buddhists are divided into a conservative Theravada School (Doctrine of the Elders) and a liberal Mahayana School (Great Vehicle). Most other factions are considered part of the Mahayana tradition.

- Mahayana Buddhism deemphasizes the historical Buddha, since everyone has the potential to become a Buddha. It also allows the integration of other religious practices into Buddhism.

- Vajrayana School (Diamond Vehicle), headed by the Dalai Lama, incorporates esoteric practices borrowed from Tibetan shamanism and Hindu tantric meditation techniques.

- Zen Buddhism promotes the idea of mindfulness and focuses on creating a "quickening of the spirit" (*satori* experience) through martial arts, aesthetics, riddles (*koan*), and so on.

- Folk Buddhism, as practiced in the majority world, incorporates the veneration of bodhisattvas. A bodhisattva is a compassionate Buddha who comes back from the realm of nirvana to live in *samsara* to lead others into the path of enlightenment. Popular bodhisattvas:

  Avalokitesvara: Often depicted as a god with multiple hands. In Tibet, the Dalai Lama is believed to be the reincarnation of Avalokitesvara. In China, he is worshipped as a white-robed deity, Guan-yin, who has the power to grant children.

  Amitabha/Amida: A bodhisattva who lives in a paradise called Pure Land. Everyone who praises his name, *Namu Amida Butsu* (Praise Amida Buddha), will be reborn into Pure Land by his grace.

  Maitreya: The one who will come

into the world at the end of this age to establish an era in which everyone becomes enlightened. In China, he is portrayed as "Budai"—the famous laughing Buddha.

• A Buddhist may consider Jesus to be one of the many sentient beings in whom the Buddha nature is realized. In that sense, He is one of the many Buddhas who have passed through this world.

• Jesus can also be considered as an enlightened bodhisattva who, instead of choosing to enter the realm of nirvana, decided to come back to the world in order to help others achieve enlightenment.

READ

"The Suffering Savior"
Chapter 3, *The Unknown God*

REFLECTION QUESTIONS

1. Religious scholars often compare the teachings of Jesus and Buddha. How are they similar? How are they different?

2. What is the Buddhist solution to the problem of suffering? How would you respond to this solution?

3. How is Western Buddhism different from Folk Buddhism practiced in the majority world?

4. How is heaven understood in Buddhism? How is it different from the Christian understanding of the same?

5. How is the Christian idea of "savior" similar to or different from the Buddhist concept of bodhisattva?

EXERCISE

Visit a Buddhist temple and observe their religious rituals. If Buddhism does not believe in gods, why are the devotees bowing down in front of the idols?

Talk to Buddhists from different ethnic and cultural backgrounds. How do their perceptions of salvation differ from one another? How much of what you hear from them can be considered part of Buddha's original teachings?

MODULE 4

UNDERSTANDING
SIKHISM

OBJECTIVE

This module presents Sikhism as a hybrid religion evolved out of the theology of Islam and the cosmology of Hinduism. It also examines how the Sikh concept of the word becoming the lord reflects the Christian idea of the Word becoming flesh.

SCRIPTURE

John 1:1–5, 14–18

WATCH

Understanding Sikhism
(Module 4: The Mosaic Course)

KEY POINTS

- Sikhism emerged at the turn of the 16th century AD in Punjab, a region now split between India and Pakistan. Today, it is the fifth-largest religion in the world.

- Guru Nanak (AD 1469–1539), the founder of Sikhism, was born into a Hindu family. His idea of God was deeply influenced by the theology of his Muslim tutor.

- Nanak received a revelation from God that said, "There is neither Hindu nor Muslim." Those who followed his teachings came to be known as *sikhs* (learners or disciples).

- After Guru Nanak, the Sikhs had nine more Gurus. The tenth Guru, Guru Gobind Singh, appointed the Sikh scripture *Adi Granth* as the final and the eternal Guru. It is now known as *Guru Granth Sahib*.

- An initiated Sikh male wears a designated attire, which can be best described as half Muslim (i.e., the turban on his head) and half Hindu (i.e., the tunic of a sadhu). His attire is identified by the "5 Ks":

  Kesh or hair: the hair and beard are uncut and are tucked inside the Turban.

  Kansha or comb: to groom the hair and the beard.

Kirpan or sword: a small dagger used for self-defense.

Karha or bracelet: worn on the right hand like a military dog tag.

Kacha or long shorts: the undergarment used by soldiers.

- The *theology* of Sikhism is shaped by the strict monotheistic doctrine of Islam, while its *cosmology* is grounded on the Hindu belief in reincarnation.

- According to the reincarnation theory in Eastern religions, we live in *samsara*—an endless cycle of life, death, and rebirth driven by the law of karma.

- Karma is a psychic energy created by the actions of an individual. Good actions create positive karma and bad actions create negative karma. The net sum of the accumulated karma decides how one is going to be reborn into the next life.

- An individual soul transmigrates from one body to another through six realms of reincarnation: heaven, human world, animal world, realm of the titans, realm of the ghosts, and hell. (*Refer to the elevator analogy in the video.*)

- Heaven and hell are impermanent states of existence. True liberation comes from escaping the samsara cycle into an alternate reality, which is called *moksha* in Hinduism, *nirvana* in Buddhism, and *sachkandh* in Sikhism.

- In Hinduism, one attains moksha by renouncing worldly life and living an ascetic life as a yogi. In Buddhism, nirvana is achieved by following the middle way. In Sikhism, one enters sachkandh by leading a life of devotion to God.

- The God of Sikhism has no name. He is addressed as *Sat nam* or True Name, and he is also described as *Sat Guru* (True Guru), *Wah Guru* (Wonderful Guru), *Ek Omkar* (One Om), and so on.

- The Sat Guru is the divine being who created the world. He is also the giver of peace and the hope of purification from all our sins. In Christianity, Jesus is the creator of the world sent by God to reveal His true nature to humanity. He brings peace and reconciliation between God and humans by redeeming the world from its sinful nature.

- A Sikh temple is called *Gurdwara* (House of the Guru). The Golden Temple in Amritsar (Punjab, India) is the religious center of Sikhism.

- Sikhs do not have official clergy. Both men and women have equal rights to perform all aspects of the religious service.

- An important part of the service is *langar*—a community kitchen that serves meals for everyone.

- The Sikh scripture, Guru Granth Sahib, is literally the current Guru of Sikhism. It is a compilation of devotional hymns written by many authors, including some non-Sikhs.

- The Sikhs treat their scripture as a living person and use a personal title (*sahib*) to address it.

- The Guru Granth Sahib is usually carried on the devotee's head and rested under a canopy. When it is being read, a *chauri* (whisk) is waved over it like a fan. It can be consulted only during the day. By the end of the day, it is put to rest in a special bedroom like any other member of the family.

- Most Sikhs would consider Jesus a *sant* (saint)—a human who achieved enlightenment through intense devotion to God. A few may regard Him as a Guru on par with the ten Gurus of Sikhism.

• Sikhs' understanding of their scripture is analogous to the Christian belief of the Word (*Logos*) becoming flesh in the person of Jesus Christ.

• In Sikhism, God (Ek Omkar) makes himself known through his *shabad* (word). The word is revered as the last and the final Guru, treated as a living person, and addressed as *sahib* (the lord). In Christianity, God reveals Himself through the Word, which became flesh in the person of Jesus Christ, who now lives among us as Lord.

READ

"The Word Becomes the Lord"
Chapter 4, *The Unknown God*

REFLECTION QUESTIONS

1. Why are the Sikhs wrongly associated with Islamic terrorism?

2. What is the name of God in Sikhism? How is it different from that of other religions?

3. Why do the Sikhs treat their sacred scripture as a living entity?

4. Why is Sikhism considered a hybrid religion?

5. How is the doctrine of reincarnation in Sikhism different from reincarnation in Hinduism and Buddhism?

EXERCISE

Browse through a Sikh hymnal and mark the verses that describe love and grace. How are they similar to or different from Christian hymns?

Visit a Gurdwara and observe a worship service. How is this experience different from visiting a church, temple, or mosque? What is the primary focus of the service?

MODULE 5

UNDERSTANDING ISLAM

OBJECTIVE

This module focuses on the origin and evolution of Islam with a special emphasis on the life and teachings of the prophet Muhammad. It also examines how the Quran depicts Jesus Christ as a prophet who is born of a virgin, a man who never committed sin, and the Messiah who is going to come back at the end of this age.

SCRIPTURE

Colossians 1:15–20; 2:8–10

WATCH

Understanding Islam
(Module 5: The Mosaic Course)

KEY POINTS

- Islam emerged out of a political vacuum created by the constant battles between the Byzantine (Christian) and Persian (predominantly Zoroastrian) empires in sixth-century Middle East.

- Muhammad (AD 570–632) first appeared in Mecca as a social reformer who aspired to unite the Arab tribes against the invading political powers. He used religion as a unifying force to champion the idea of "one nation under God."

- According to Islam, the God that Muhammad introduced was the same God who revealed the *Torah* (Pentateuch) to the Jews and the *Injil* (Gospel) to the Christians. However, the Jews disobeyed the Torah by plotting against Jesus, and the Christians corrupted Injil through illegitimate translations. Therefore God, Muhammad claimed, revealed to him the latest and the final revelation, the Quran.

- The Meccans rejected Muhammad's message and exiled him to Medina. He formed a private army in Medina and organized guerilla warfare against the Meccans.

- Fewer than ten years later, Muhammad returned to Mecca and captured the city. Various gods (*ilahs*) of the Arab tribes were replaced by the one God (*Al-ilah* =

the God). Muhammad declared himself the last and the final prophet of this God (Allah). This was the official founding of Islam (AD 630).

- After Muhammad's death in AD 632, Islam split into two factions: *Sunnis* under Abu Bakr (Muhammad's father-in-law) and *Shi'ites* under Ali (Muhammad's son-in-law). Ali's two sons (Muhammad's grandchildren) were later murdered by the Sunnis. This started the rivalry between the Sunnis and the Shi'ites that continues even today.

- A number of lesser-known factions also exist in Islam (Sufism, Ahammadiya movement, etc.), which are considered heretical sects by mainstream Muslims.

- A person can convert to Islam by saying a prayer of confession called *shahada*, which is translated as, "There is no god

but Allah, and Muhammad is the mes-
senger of Allah."

- True Muslims follow a common creed
  often referred to as the "five pillars" of
  Islam. They recite the confession of faith
  (*shahada*); pray five times a day (*salat*);
  faithfully give a percentage of their earn-
  ings to the poor (*zakat*); fast during the
  month of Ramadan (*sawm*); and aspire to
  make the ultimate pilgrimage to Mecca
  (*hajj*), a journey that each Muslim is
  recommended to make at least once in
  a lifetime.

- According to Islam, the Quran is the lit-
  eral word of God descended from heaven.
  Muhammad did not write the Quran; he
  only recited the verses as he heard them
  from the angel of Allah.

- Jesus is arguably the most mentioned
  person in the Quran. His mother, Mary,

is the only woman to be mentioned by name.

• According to the Quran, Jesus is a prophet who brought the Injil (Gospel) from Allah (Sura 5:46).

• Jesus was born of a virgin by the Spirit of God, without a human father (Sura 3:45–47; 19:16–22).

• Jesus led a sinless life (Sura 19:19).

• Jesus did many miracles (including speaking from His crib as an infant) (Sura 2:87; 3:46).

• Jesus is addressed as the Messiah (Sura 4:157), the Word from God (Sura 4:171; 3:45), and the Spirit from God (Sura 4:171).

- According to the Quran, Jesus did not die on the cross; instead, He was taken directly into heaven (Sura 4:157, 158).

- Muslims anticipate Jesus' second coming to establish a world of peace in complete submission to God.

READ

"The Man Who Became a Sign"
Chapter 5, *The Unknown God*

REFLECTION QUESTIONS

1. What are the sociopolitical issues that contributed to the birth of Islam?

2. How does the Islamic understanding of the Quran differ from the Christian understanding of the Bible?

3. Which are the different factions within Islam? What are the major disputes between them?

4. Compare and contrast the portrayal of Jesus in the Quran and in the Bible. How do you explain the differences between them?

5. What are some of the Islamic theories about the crucifixion of Jesus?

EXERCISE

On a world map, identify the countries that are considered Islamic Republics. Check the growth statistics of other (non-Muslim) religious traditions in these countries. What are your inferences?

If possible, attend the Eid al-Adha celebrations of a Muslim community. Try to understand the meaning of sacrifice according to Islam. Why was a sacrifice necessary to ransom the son of Abraham in the story of Eid al-Adha?

MODULE 6

UNDERSTANDING JUDAISM

OBJECTIVE

This module outlines the beliefs and practices of contemporary (Rabbinic) Judaism in contrast to the biblical (Priestly) Judaism. It also illustrates how Jesus is revealed in the Hebrew Scriptures as the Messiah who is both a triumphant king and a suffering servant.

SCRIPTURE

Deuteronomy 6:4–9

WATCH

Understanding Judaism
(Module 6: The Mosaic Course)

KEY POINTS

- Judaism is the smallest of all major living religions, yet it is the mother of the two largest religions in the world (Christianity and Islam).

- In general, Jews believe that people inherit their religion. A person born to Jewish parents is considered a Jew even if he or she does not practice Judaism, whereas a non-Jew who observes the Jewish law may still be considered a Gentile.

- What we find in the Bible is Priestly Judaism, which regards priests as the intercessors between God and His people. The destruction of the second temple in AD 60 paved the way for Rabbinic Judaism, in which rabbis assume the role of the priests and *halachah* (the Jewish law) becomes a means to reconciliation with God.

- Orthodox Judaism adheres to rabbinic interpretations of halachah and promotes strict observance of the Jewish law. Conservative Judaism caters to the demands of cultural changes while also emphasizing the value of traditional laws and rituals. Reform Judaism focuses mostly on ethical aspects of Judaism rather than its theological doctrines.

- Messianic Judaism considers Jesus as the Messiah and integrates Jewish customs and practices into their religious services.

- The Jewish Scripture is called the *Tanach*, which is a combination of *Torah* (the Pentateuch), *Nevi'im* (the Prophets), and *Ketuvim* (the writings).

- Judaism is a religion of the covenant. Technically, anyone can accept the Jewish religion through a binding ritual of consent in which the person affirms faith in the covenants God established with Abraham (Genesis 12), Moses (Exodus 20), and David (2 Samuel 7).

- The concept of the Promised Land is central to Jewish theology. The Jewish law is integrally connected to the land.

- The Jews do not follow a formal creed. However, "The Thirteen Principles of Faith," developed by Rabbi Maimonides (AD 1135–1204), serves as a general guide to their belief system.

- Jews observe *tzedakah* (tithe), *kosher* (dietary code), and *shabbat* (rest on the seventh day of the week).

- Jews keep a *Mezuza* (a container in which Deuteronomy 6:4–9 and 11:13–21 are written on parchments) on the doorpost.

- Male Jews use a *kippah* (skull cap), *tefflin* (phylacteries worn on the arms and the head), and a *tallit* (shawl) during their prayer times.

- Because Jesus taught from the Jewish Scriptures, observed Jewish rituals, and faithfully practiced the Jewish law, most Jews consider Jesus to have been a rabbi.

- The Jewish festivals such as *Yom Kippur* (Day of Atonement) and *Pesach* (Passover) rely heavily on the idea of sacrifice (*korban*) as the necessary prerequisite for the forgiveness of sins. Christians believe that the animal sacrifices in the Hebrew

Scriptures are symbolic depictions of Jesus' sacrifice on the cross.

- In *Nostra Aetate* (1965), the Catholic Church recognized the continuing validity of God's covenant with Israel, and now most evangelical churches offer unmitigated support of the Jewish nation.

- The Jews are waiting for a Messiah (this is the twelfth principle of the Thirteen Principles of Faith) who will come to the world in order to restore the nation of Israel and reestablish its political sovereignty.

- Rabbinic texts struggle with two conflicting portrayals of the Messiah in the Hebrew Scriptures—a triumphant king (Messiah ben David) and a suffering servant (Messiah ben Joseph). Are they indeed two different Messiahs, or simply two faces of the same Messiah?

• The Jewish declaration: "To Do the Will of Our Father in Heaven: Toward a Partnership between Jews and Christians" (December 2015), signed by many prominent Orthodox rabbis, suggests, "Jesus brought a double goodness to the world.... On the one hand he strengthened the Torah of Moses majestically" and on the other hand, "he removed idols from the nations," instilling them "firmly with moral traits." Therefore, "Christianity is neither an accident nor an error, but the willed divine outcome and gift to the nations."

READ

"The Pierced Messiah"
Chapter 6, *The Unknown God*

REFLECTION QUESTIONS

1. How is the Judaism of the Bible different from the Judaism that is being practiced today?

2. What is Messianic Judaism?

3. How is the Jewish understanding of the Messiah similar to or different from the Christian perception of the Messiah?

4. Do the Hebrew Scriptures picture God in human form?

5. What is the significance of animal sacrifices in Judaism? How does the ritual of sacrifice symbolize the death of Jesus on the cross?

EXERCISE

Browse through news articles related to current events in Israel. How do they resonate with the Jewish understanding of Israel as the Promised Land? How would you evaluate these events in light of Jewish hopes and dreams?

Attend a Passover celebration in a Jewish home. How is it similar to or different from the Holy Communion that Christians celebrate in churches?

MODULE 7

WHAT'S SO GOOD ABOUT THE GOOD NEWS?

OBJECTIVE

This module proposes the idea that Jesus of Nazareth is the historical fulfillment of the Christ figures in pre-Christian traditions. It also illustrates the uniqueness and significance of the Christian message in contrast to that of other world religions.

SCRIPTURE

Romans 1:16–17

WATCH

What Is So Good about the Good News?
(Module 7: The Mosaic Course)

KEY POINTS

- Christianity is the only religion that calls its message the "good news." The Christian message is not what Jesus said or did, but it is who He is. The gospel, unlike the messages of other religions, is not merely a truth-claim; it is Truth personified.

- Religion is the story of humanity's search for God, but Christianity is the story of God's search for humanity. According to the Bible, we are created in the image and likeness of God. When we lost His image and likeness in the Garden of Eden, God took our image and likeness in Christ, in order to reestablish the relationship. It is the ultimate good news presented by Christianity.

- Jesus redefined religion in terms of relationship. Most religions conceptualize the idea of a Creator God who is indifferent to the world of His creation. Jesus, on the other hand, revealed a Father God who invites us into an intimate relationship with Him.

- A God who is love (Father) cannot be just (Creator), and a God who is just cannot be love (in the act of forgiveness). In order to solve this cosmic dilemma, God takes the burden of our sins upon Himself on the cross of Christ and establishes a radically new relationship with humanity. Christianity, therefore, proclaims the end of religion and the beginning of a relationship.

- God accepts us not because of what we do (righteousness) but because of who we are (relationship) in Christ. Christianity thus replaces the law of karma (doing right things to become righteous) with the theology of grace (doing right things because we are deemed righteous in Christ).

- There are genuine allusions to this redemptive grace in the sacred texts of non-Christian religions. This could be the result of a primeval revelation from God to the whole of humanity, which was later distorted by human speculation and cultural appropriation.

- Christ is the ultimate revelation of God in time and space, and thus the historical culmination of the Christ figures found in other religions. This is why a Christian can affirm the fact that Jesus is the only way to God while also paying due respect to people of other religious faiths.

READ

"The Emptied God"
Chapter 7, *The Unknown God*

"The True Myth"
Chapter 8, *The Unknown God*

REFLECTION QUESTIONS

1. How do the Christ figures in world religions function as silent pointers to the historical Christ?

2. Why do Christians call Jesus the "Son of God" even though Jesus addressed Himself as the "Son of Man"? What is the difference?

3. Why can Christianity be said to be "the end of religion and the beginning of a relationship"?

4. How do you differentiate between the law of karma and the theology of grace?

5. Why did Jesus have to die for the salvation of humanity? Couldn't God have forgiven us all at His will?

EXERCISE

Ask people of different religious faiths how they address God in their prayers. How is it different from the Lord's Prayer, which addresses God as "Our Father"?

Browse through the sacred texts of different religions to see if they contain a map. What is the theological significance of the maps or geographical cartograms you find in most versions of the Bible?

BONUS MODULE

JESUS ACCORDING TO ATHEISM

The Mosaic Course was originally conceived as an attempt to develop a Christian response to world religions. In the process of framing the course, we became increasingly aware of the fact that the definition of religion can be extended to include a wide spectrum of belief systems, including a belief in the non-existence of God.

Even those who describe themselves as atheists, agnostics, or secular humanists consider Jesus to be a person of significant influence in our postmodern culture. They see

Him not only as a thinker who deconstructs the dominant religious narratives of the culture, but also as an activist who advocates the cause of the marginal voices in our society.

In this bonus module of the Mosaic Course, we present some redemptive bridges between Christianity and atheism—the "anti-religious religion" of our culture.

> *"Atheism is more doctrinal than*
> *any of the great religions.*
> *By definition, atheists agree on the*
> *dogma that there is no god,*
> *just as monotheists agree on the*
> *dogma that there is one.*
> *Belief is their preoccupation."*
> **Stephen Prothero**
> *(God Is Not One: The Eight Rival*
> *Religions That Run the World—and*
> *Why Their Differences Matter)*

OBJECTIVE

The purpose of this bonus module is to explore the under-lying principles of atheism, which presents itself as an anti-religious religion in our culture. It also attempts to understand Jesus from the perspective of a secular humanist and examines how Christ is revealed in secular imagination outside the sphere of religion.

SCRIPTURE

1 Corinthians 3:19–20

WATCH

Understanding Atheism
(Bonus Module: The Mosaic Course)

KEY POINTS

- Secular humanism—an amalgamation of a wide spectrum of belief systems ranging from atheism to agnosticism—functions like a religion in our society. The U.S. Supreme Court decreed in 1961 that secular humanism should be treated as a religion and should receive First Amendment protections like all other religions.

- Atheists admit that the existence of God is a hypothesis that cannot be factually disproved. The presupposition of atheism, therefore, is founded on a system of belief like other non-theistic religions, such as Buddhism.

- Atheists believe in the existence of a natural law that governs the universe. A law, by definition, can be conceived only by a mind that transcends the universe.

- Three manifestations of Atheist doctrines:

  God may exist, but He doesn't care about us. If an all-powerful, all-loving God exists, there should be no suffering in this world. Therefore, even if God exists, He is indifferent to our world, and hence is of no use to us.

God may exist, but we don't need Him. We can be good without God and build an ideal society without the divine mandates imposed by religions. Therefore, even if God exists, He is irrelevant to our existence in the world.

God may exist, but we must get rid of Him. Religious violence poses an imminent threat to human existence. Therefore, even if God exists, we should eradicate Him from public consciousness.

- God has put eternity in the hearts of humanity (Ecclesiastes 3:11). A deep longing for immortality and a craving for transcendent values haunt us all, including the atheists. As a result, whenever we try to eradicate religion, it mutates into various forms of new (age) spirituality.

- A significant majority of the people who self-identify themselves as "nones" (a person with no religious affiliation) are not atheists; they are looking for "spirituality" in secular spaces.

- Since all human beings are created in the image and likeness of God, it is natural to assume that God presents Himself in human imagination, even outside the sphere of religion.

- Scholars have long observed patterns of thought common to all humanity, which influence and even shape our cultural narratives—be it philosophy, art, or religion. Carl Jung, one of the founding fathers of modern psychology, called the patterns "archetypes of the collective unconscious."

- One such archetype is a Christ figure, a symbolic character that exhibits the fundamental nature of Christ's redemptive work in film, literature, art, and so on.

Christ figures found in secular imagination can be considered products of the subconscious theological memory of the culture.

- Jesus on the cross typifies the ultimate Christ archetype. Here is the best possible human being going through the worst possible tragedy for the sake of others. Jesus Christ can therefore be considered the historical culmination of these mythical archetypes in the popular culture.

- A fraction of atheists might still doubt the existence of the historical Christ, but there is a general consensus among scholars that a person named Jesus lived in first-century Palestine, that the Roman procurator Pontius Pilate crucified Him, and that His followers claimed that He came back from the dead.

• Although Jesus' divinity is disputed, the compelling nature of His humanity appeals to most atheists:

> He was a rebel who challenged the foundational structures of the organized religion of His time.
>
> He was a moral advocate who championed the cause of the poor, the oppressed, and the disenfranchised in society.
>
> He was a great storyteller who articulated abstract truths in metaphorical language, touching a deep chord of resonance with the human heart.

• The suffering God on the cross identifies with the ultimate predicament of humanity, including those who do not believe in His existence. Some would even argue that Jesus Himself became an "atheist" when He felt separated from God for a moment on the cross and cried, "My God, My God, why have You forsaken Me?" (Matthew 27:46).

- The humanity of Jesus can thus be considered a missiological bridge to His divinity. According to the "trilemma" theory of C. S. Lewis, a man who said and did what Jesus said and did should be considered either a liar or a lunatic … unless He really is the Lord.

READ

"The True Myth"
Reread Chapter 8, *The Unknown God*

REFLECTION QUESTIONS

1. What do you think about the statement, "There are no atheists; only believers and heretics"?

2. What are some of the "mutated" forms of religion in our culture?

3. What is a Christ figure? How does it present itself in popular culture?

4. Why is the humanity of Jesus appealing to an atheist?

5. What is the trilemma theory of C. S. Lewis? How can it act as a bridge between Jesus' humanity and His divinity?

EXERCISE

Identify some of the spiritual instincts of your friends who consider themselves atheists or secular humanists (e.g., moral advocacy, their craving for afterlife, etc.).

Pick a story of your choice and spot the archetypes in its narrative arc. Do any of them resemble a Christ figure?

APPENDIX

JESUS ACCORDING TO OTHER RELIGIONS

We have limited the content of the Mosaic Course to the six major living religions (including Christianity) in the world. Of course, there are many others that are either considered minor, on account of the number of adherents, or local, in terms of their geographic reach.

However, we believe a cursory knowledge of two Chinese religions will be of interest to our readers, considering their increased prominence in the Western World.

SHANG DI–THE ONE GOD OF ANCIENT CHINA

This is not widely known in the West, but the ancient religion of China was monotheistic. It centered on the worship of a supreme God, Shang Di (the Emperor of Heaven). He was never represented in the form of an image or idol, like the God of the Bible is. The Emperors of China were revered as the mediators between the people and Shang Di, and they used to perform "border sacrifices"—a ritual that closely resembles the sacrifices in the Bible—to reconcile the relationship between them.

The Altar of Heaven in which these sacrifices took place still stands today. The Temple of Heaven, dedicated to Shang Di, can be found in Beijing.

The worship of Shang Di eventually shifted its focus from the personhood of the Lord of Heaven to the idea of heaven (*Tien*) itself. Eventually, it was overshadowed by the myriad of gods and goddesses imported by Buddhism.

However, the remnants of this High God still persist in Chinese culture. Many believe that even the ancient Chinese language was deeply influenced by the worship of Shang Di. For example, the Chinese calligraphy for the word *righteousness* is a combination of the following two symbols:

羊 + 我 = 義
Lamb   **Me**   **Righteousness**

The etymology of this Chinese word, according to Christian missionaries, reflects the biblical notion that righteousness is achieved by covering oneself with the blood of a sacrificial lamb. Many Christians in China consider Shang Di to be the Chinese manifestation of the God of the Bible. In some versions of the Chinese Bible, the word *God* is rendered as "Shang Di."

CONFUCIANISM

The origin of this philosophy is attributed to the great Chinese teacher Confucius (551–479 BC). Confucianism is considered more of a wisdom tradition than a religion.

The sacred scripture of Confucianism, the Analects,[2] discusses a system of personal and social ethics centered on humans, not on God. Confucius never claimed himself to be God or a prophet, but he believed what he proclaimed was the "ordinance of heaven."

Confucius acknowledged the existence of gods and demons in Chinese folklore, but his focus was on the flourishing of a person in familial and societal contexts. Family is the basic unit of society, and familial duty is the supreme virtue.

Instead of worshipping the Emperor of Heaven (*Shang Di*), Confucius taught that one should find his or her way to heaven (*Tien*) by accumulating *ren*[3] (humanity or benevolence). Heaven is not merely a celestial place in Confucianism; it is the origin of all virtues and the dispenser of all honor, wealth, and glory in the universe.

A Confucian would consider Jesus to be a *Jun-zi*, a complete and perfect man who embodies the nature of heaven. Jun-zi is often described by the phrase "Inner Sage and Outer King." An Inner Sage achieves perfection of ethical virtues within his own self, and the Outer King performs great and mighty deeds in the physical world.

Such an ideal man will build an ideal society. The laws of this society will flow naturally from the moral character of the virtuous man, not from written codes and regulations. In the end, he will fulfill the ancient Chinese dream of "Great Unity" (*da-tong*) between people and heaven.

DAOISM

This religion receives its name from the principle of *Dao*, a universal spiritual energy that is said to manifest itself in two complementary forces, *Yin* and *Yang*. The ultimate goal of a Daoist is to achieve union with Dao by living in complete harmony with these natural forces of the universe.

Tai Chi, a popular contemplative practice that is becoming increasingly popular in the West, is a tool to perfect this process. *Te* is usually interpreted as the awareness of Dao, and *Ch'i* the psychic energy that connects us to the universe. By practicing Tai Chi, one would be able to align the vital energy of his or her body with that of Dao.

A mythical figure named Lao Tzu (Laozi) is believed to be the founder of Daoism, and the authorship of *Dao De Ching*, the foundational text of Daoism, is attributed to Laozi. However, his existence is highly disputed by historians.

Although Dao is not a personal god and is not worshipped as such, folk Daoism has many deities, most of which are borrowed from indigenous Chinese religions and Buddhism. Dao is evidently different from the Christian God, but it is interesting to note that, in many Chinese versions of the Bible, the Greek word *Logos* (translated as *Word* in English) is translated as "Dao."

The Chinese translation of John 1:1 would therefore read, "In the beginning was Dao, Dao was with God and Dao was God." In that sense, Jesus can be considered the embodiment of Dao, the creator and sustainer of the cosmos. All things in the universe are interconnected and unified in Dao. "All things came into being through Him, and apart from Him nothing came into being that has come into being" (John 1:3).

Q&A

IS JESUS THE ONLY WAY?

Do you believe Jesus is the only way to God?
Absolutely! Jesus stated it unequivocally: "No one comes to the Father but through Me" (John 14:6). Peter reiterated it even more forcefully: "There is salvation in no one else, for there is no other name under heaven that has been given among men by which we must be saved" (Acts 4:12).

But it seems you are saying that other religions can also lead us to God. Isn't that universalism?

We do not say other religions can lead us to God. All we are saying is that there could be redemptive revelations in other religions that have the "potential" to lead us to *Jesus Christ*—these are two different things.

What then is the point of Christianity? It still sounds like universalism.

Other world religions possess elements of "general revelation," but Christianity presents the world's only "particular revelation," in which we encounter the ultimate self-disclosure of God in Jesus Christ, "the image of the invisible God" (Colossians 1:15). This proposition emphasizes the exclusivity of Jesus Christ while also respecting the traces of general revelation that might be available in other cultures and religions.

Isn't a Christ who is present in all religions still a heresy and a deception of New Age spirituality?

What we assert is that Christ is *not* present in all religions. He is present only in Christianity. What other religions may have is a "Christ figure"—a hint, outline, or foreshadowing of the sublime picture of a redeeming savior—which has the potential to point people to the historical Christ (Jesus of Nazareth), who is revealed in Christianity alone. What

New Age spirituality talks about is a "Cosmic Christ," an abstract concept that has no connection to historical realities.

Paul knew very well that the unknown god in Athens was actually a pagan deity with no direct connection to Christianity. Yet he used this Christ figure as a communication key to invite his listeners to the true Christ, who is revealed only in Christianity. In the same way, we can build missiological bridges with our neighbors of other faiths using the partial revelations embedded in their own religious traditions.

If all religions lead people to Jesus, why should we share the gospel with anyone?

We do not say that all religions lead to Jesus Christ. All we are saying is that there *could* be redeemable elements in these religions, and that these elements may have the *potential* to direct people to Jesus Christ.

The Christ-event revealed in Christianity is decisive for human salvation. This is why all must come to Christ in order to be saved and receive eternal life. People may encounter spiritual experiences through other religions, but only in Christianity does God present Himself in the form of a person and invite us into a relationship with

Him. This is the Good News that Christians are called to share with others.

For more Questions and Answers, please visit

www.themosaiccourse.org

NOTES

1. Moltmann's essay "Is 'Pluralistic Theology' Useful for the Dialogue of World Religions?" challenges the views of John Hick and Paul F. Knitter.

2. The Sacred Scriptures of Confucianism, "Four Books," consist of the following other books, as well (a) The Golden Mean, (b) The Great Learning, and (c) Mencius, a text authored by philosopher Mencius, who was a devoted follower of Confucius.

3. The five cardinal virtues in Confucianism are *ren* (benevolence), *yi* (righteousness), *li* (rules of propriety or decorum), *zhi* (wisdom), and *xin* (fidelity or faithfulness).

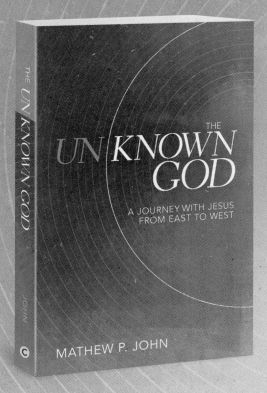